Let's Learn About D

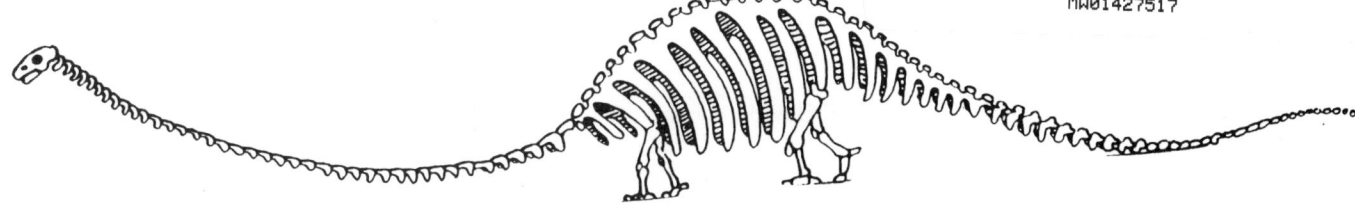

Before We Begin

Conduct a group discussion to find out how much your students already know (or think they know) about dinosaurs. Make a list of questions they have about dinosaurs on a chart. Post this in the classroom. Add answers and new questions as they come up.

This discussion will provide you with an opportunity to note any misinformation you need to address while teaching this unit.

Using Library Books

Share as much factual information from these books and other sources as is appropriate for your students.

Nonfiction:
Bones, Bones, Dinosaur Bones by Byron Barton; Crowell, 1990.
Digging Up Dinosaurs by Aliki; Harper, 1988.
Dinosaurs (Eyewitness Books) by David Norman & Angela Milner; Knopf, 1989.
Dinosaurs, Dinosaurs by Byron Barton; Crowell, 1989.
Fossils Tell of Long Ago by Aliki; Harper, 1990.
A Gallery of Dinosaurs and Other Early Reptiles by David Peters; Knopf, 1989.
The Littlest Dinosaurs by Bernard Most; Harcourt, 1989.
The Magic School Bus: In the Time of the Dinosaurs by Joanna Cole; Scholastic Inc., 1994.
The Rourke Dinosaur Dictionary by Joseph Hincks; Rourke, 1990.
My Visit to the Dinosaurs by Aliki; Harper & Row, 1985.
New Questions and Answers About Dinosaurs by Seymour Simon; Morrow Junior Books, 1990.

Fiction:
Danny and the Dinosaur by Syd Hoff; Harper, 1985.
Dinosaurs Beware by Marc Brown & Stephen Krensky; Little, 1990.
Dinosaur Bob and His Adventure with the Family Lazardo by Joyce Williams; Harper, 1988.
Four and Twenty Dinosaurs by Bernard Most; Harper, 1990.
Patrick's Dinosaurs by Carol Carrick; Clarion, 1983.
What Happened to Patrick's Dinosaurs? by Carol Carrick; Ticknor & Fields, 1986.

© 1996 Evan-Moor Corp.   Dinosaurs EMC 253

Dinosaurs

Long, long ago
When the earth was new
Dinosaurs walked
and swam and flew.

Allosaurus
Triceratops
Apatosaurus, too.

Iguanodon
Tyrannosaurus
To name just a few.

Long, long ago
When the earth was new
Huge dinosaurs lived
and small ones too.

Jo Ellen Moore

Note: Reproduce pages 2-11 to create a dinosaur book for each child. Read the pages together, then have children take them home to share with their families.

Long, Long Ago

Dinosaurs lived a long time ago. There aren't any alive today, so how do we know they ever lived?

No people were alive at the same time as the dinosaurs. There are no paintings or books to tell us about them. We have to try to understand dinosaurs by studying the fossils that are found.

Scientists put the dinosaur bones together like big puzzles. They can't tell what color a dinosaur was, but they can tell its shape and how big it was.

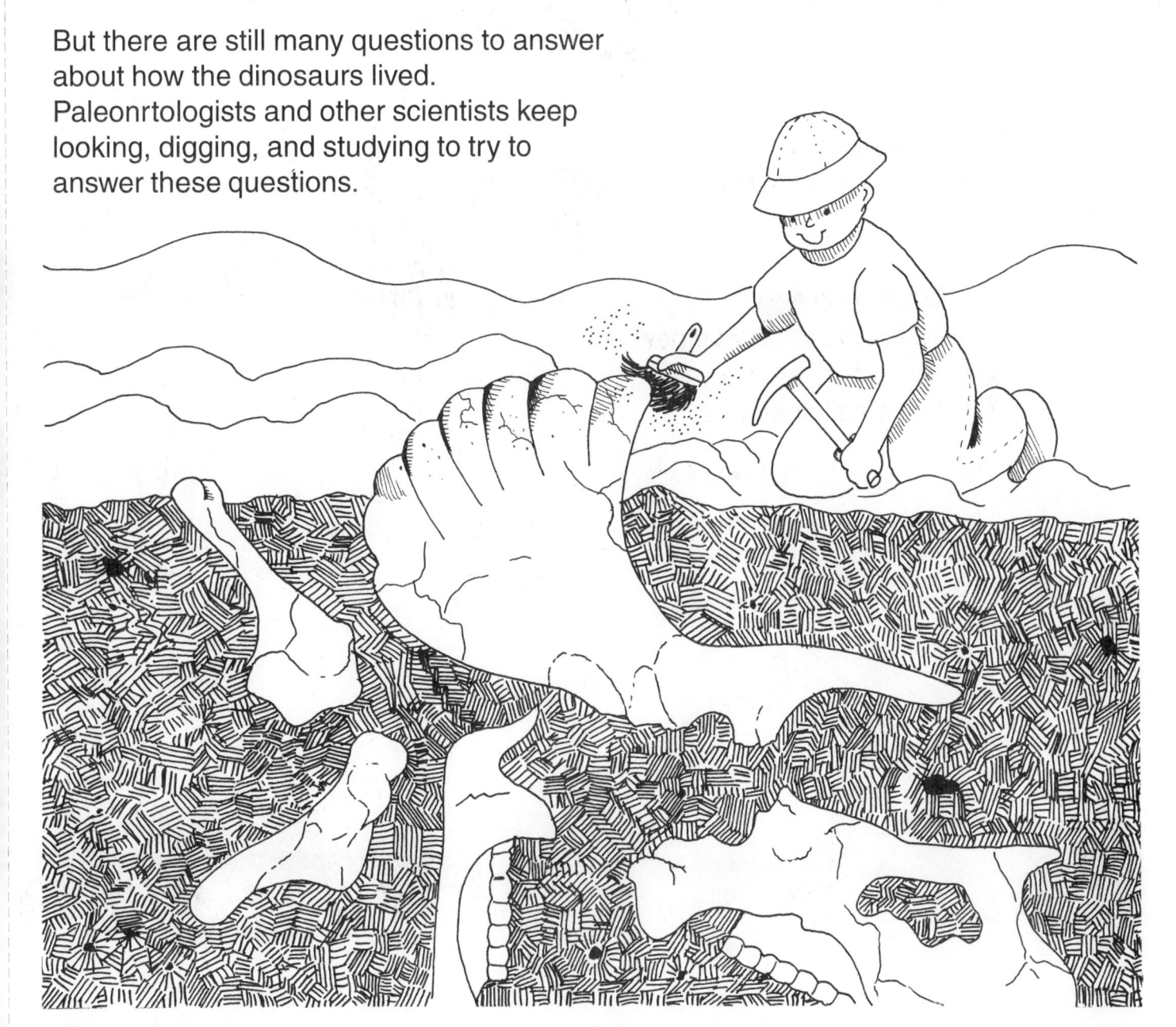

But there are still many questions to answer about how the dinosaurs lived. Paleonrtologists and other scientists keep looking, digging, and studying to try to answer these questions.

© 1996 Evan-Moor Corp.   3   Dinosaurs EMC 253

Were All Dinosaurs Huge?

Most dinosaurs you see in movies or read about in books were huge. While many dinosaurs were enormous, some were very small. Compsognathus was about the size of a chicken.

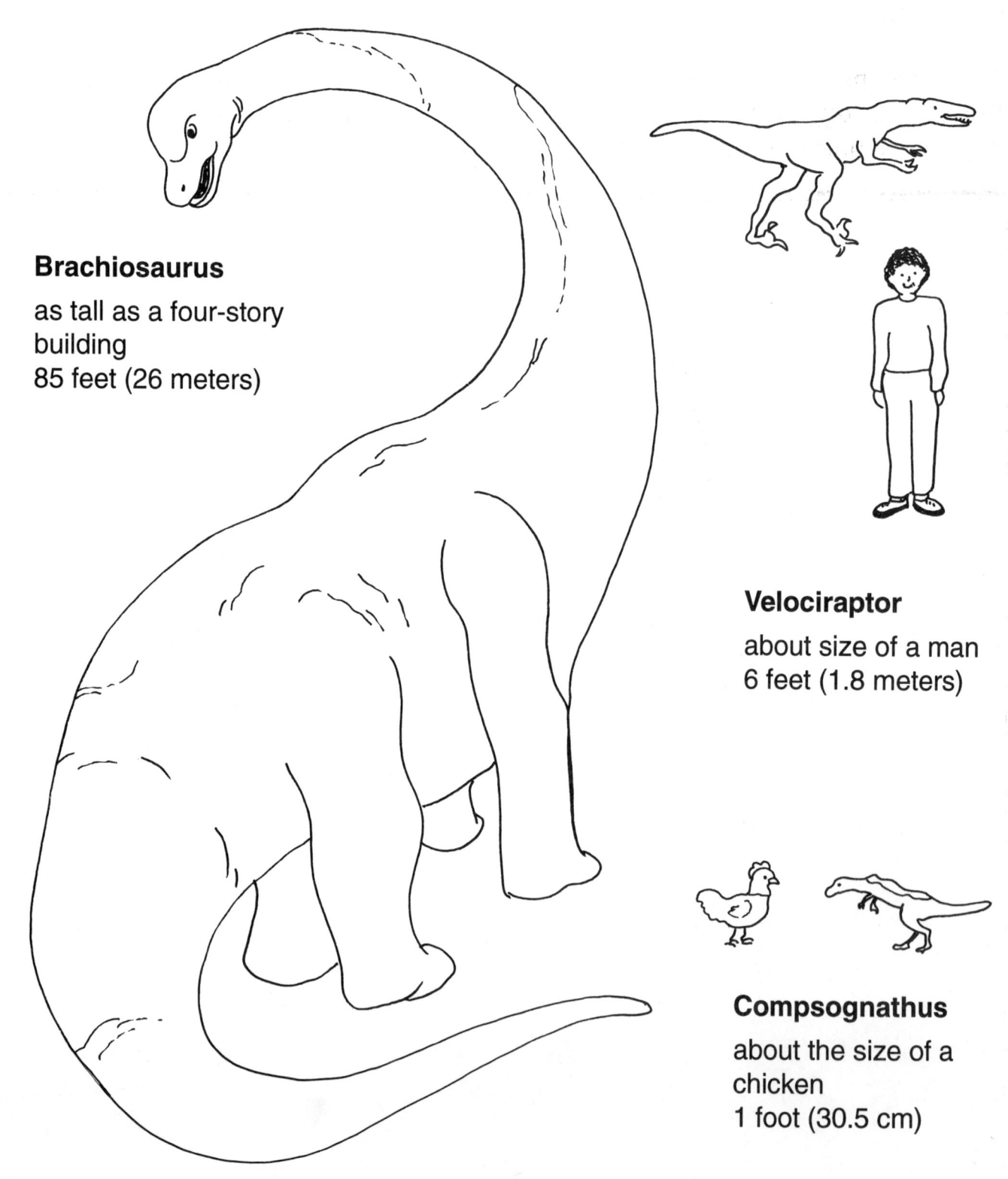

Brachiosaurus

as tall as a four-story building
85 feet (26 meters)

Velociraptor

about size of a man
6 feet (1.8 meters)

Compsognathus

about the size of a chicken
1 foot (30.5 cm)

© 1996 Evan-Moor Corp. Dinosaurs EMC 253

Note: A few scientists believe some dinosaurs may have had live babies, but currently there is not absolute proof. You may choose to discuss this possibility with your students.

Dinosaur Life Cycle

Scientists think dinosaurs laid eggs. Fossil eggs and nests have been found in several places around the world. Some of the fossil eggs contained skeletons of baby dinosaurs.

These are the eggs of one dinosaur. The mother dinosaur dug a nest in the sand. She laid her eggs in the nest and covered them with sand. The sand helped keep the eggs warm until the baby dinosaurs were ready to hatch.

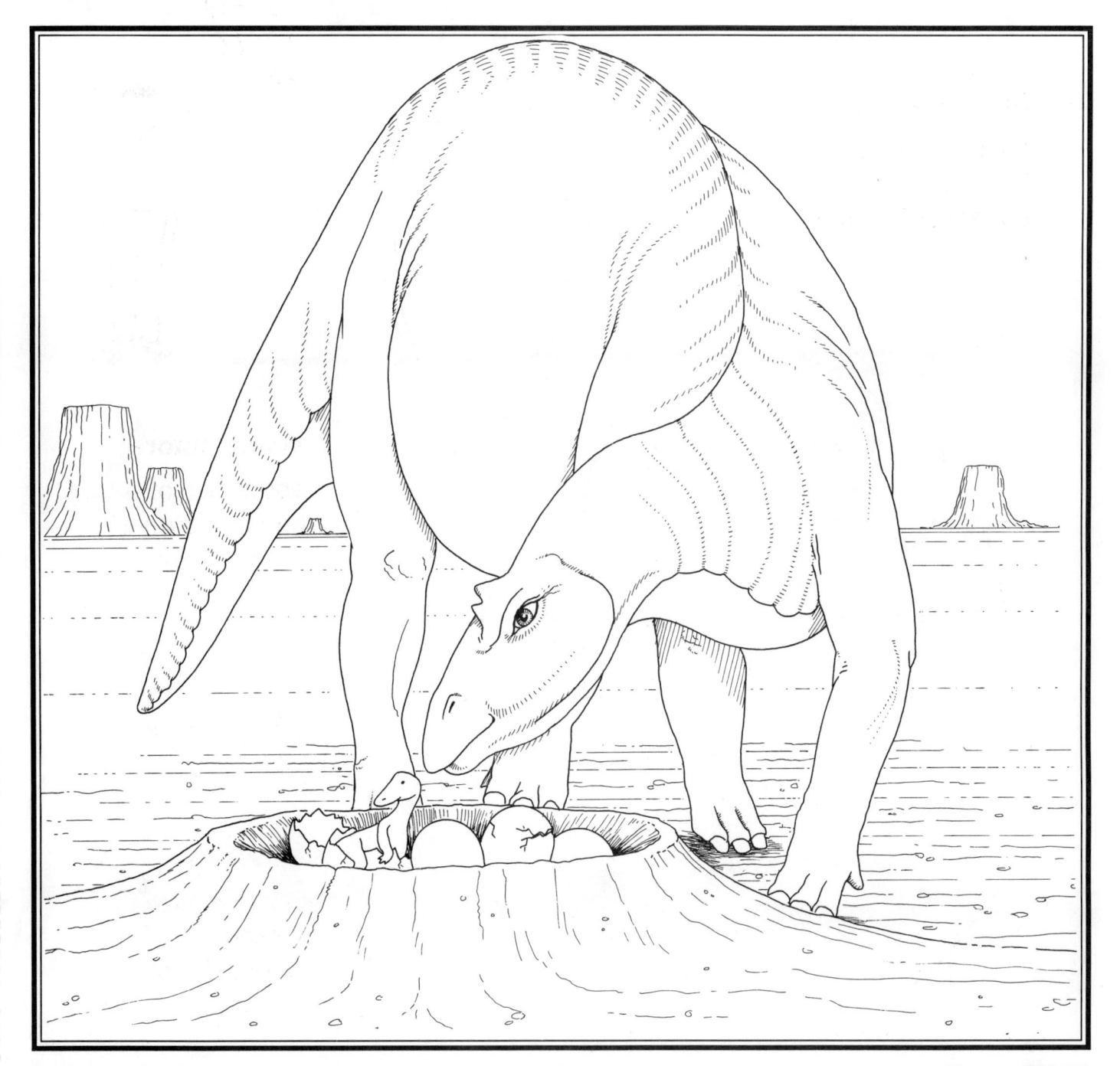

© 1996 Evan-Moor Corp. 5 Dinosaurs EMC 253

What Did Dinosaurs Eat?

Scientists can make a good guess by looking at the shape of the dinosaur's teeth.

Meat-eaters usually have teeth with sharp points and jagged edges. This helps them tear up the meat.

Plant-eaters had teeth that were smooth and flat on top for grinding plants.

Scientists think that some plant-eating dinosaurs didn't have flat surfaces on their teeth. Iguanodon had jagged teeth, but they were not sharp like the teeth of a meat-eater.

Some large plant-eaters have been found with small stones in the middle of their skeletons. Scientists think they may have swallowed the stones to help grind up their food. This is what modern birds do.

Are you a plant-eater, a meat-eater, or are you both? Circle the types of foods you eat.

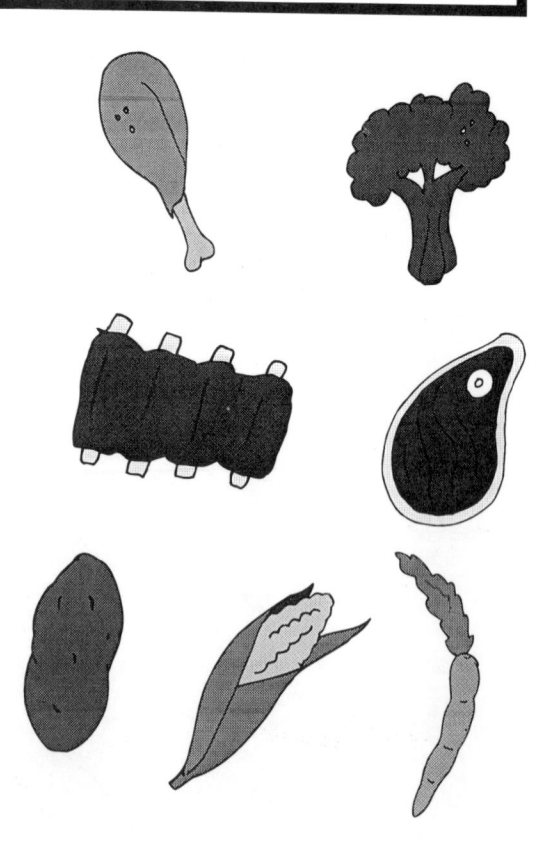

Dinosaurs in Motion

Some dinosaurs moved on two legs. Others moved on four legs.

The meat-eaters usually had short front legs and longer back legs. They moved around on the two back legs. Their tails were held out to balance their heavy heads and chests.

Plant-eaters usually had four legs about the same size. They walked around on all four legs. Some were able to raise up on two legs to reach for food up in trees.

There were also prehistoric animals that flew in the air and that swam in the water.

How did dinosaurs protect themselves?

Each kind of dinosaur had its own ways of protecting itself.

Some frightened other dinosaurs with their big size.
Some could run fast.
Small dinosaurs could also hide in little spaces.
Some dinosaurs had sharp claws and teeth.
Some had hard plates on their bodies.
Some had pointed horns to fight with.
Dinosaurs that could fly could escape danger in that way.

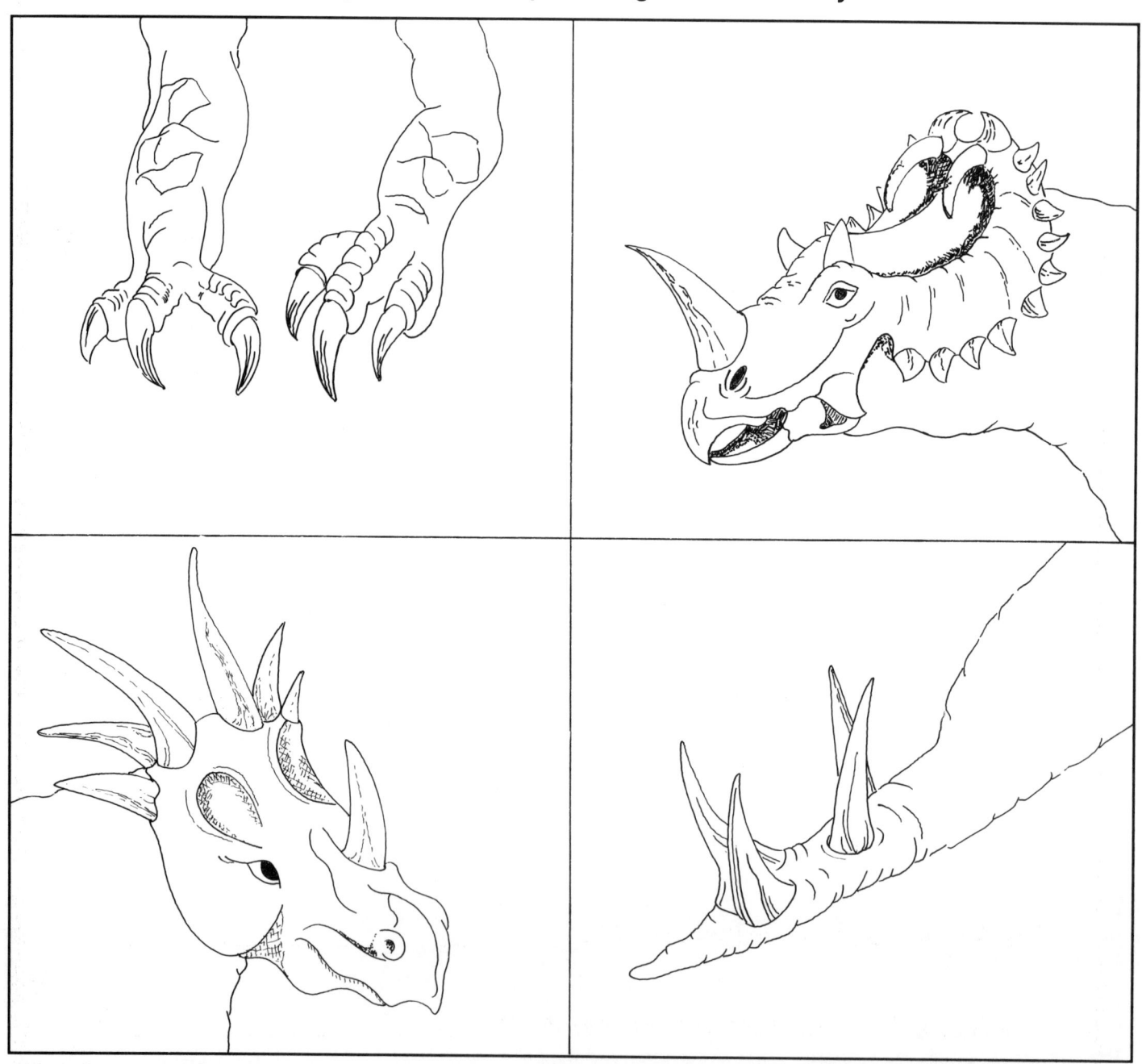

Dinosaurs

Other Prehistoric Animals

Dinosaurs are not the only animals that lived long ago.
Other kinds of animals lived at the same time as the dinosaur.
Some prehistoric animals lived after the dinosaurs diappeared.

Look at the animals on this page.
Do they remind you of any animals that are alive today?

Woolly Mammoth

Archaeopteryx

Saber-Toothed Tiger

The Woolly Mammoth reminds me of the _____ .

The Archaeopteryx reminds me of the _____ .

The Saber-Toothed Tiger reminds me of the _____ .

© 1996 Evan-Moor Corp.   Dinosaurs EMC 253

Why Did the Dinosaurs Disappear?

Scientists do not agree on what caused dinosaurs to become extinct. They have many ideas, but there is no proof of what really happened.

Some scientists think that only the large dinosaurs became extinct. They believe that the small dinosaurs gradually changed into animals that are alive today.

Many scientists now think that the dinosaurs died because the climate became too hot and plants died. Without food, the plant-eaters died. The meat-eaters then had less food to eat. After a time, the weather became very cold, and the rest of the large dinosaurs died.

Scientists don't agree on what caused this change. Was it a giant comet hitting the earth? Were there eruptions of large volcanoes? Scientists are still trying to find the answer.

What do you think happened? Draw a picture to show your answer.

Have All the Dinosaurs Disappeared?

Some scientists think that the small meat-eating dinosaurs are the ancestors of modern birds.

The skeletons of the little dinosaur compsognathus and the first bird archaeopteryx look very much alike. The biggest difference is feathers. Archaeopteryx had them. Compsognathus didn't.

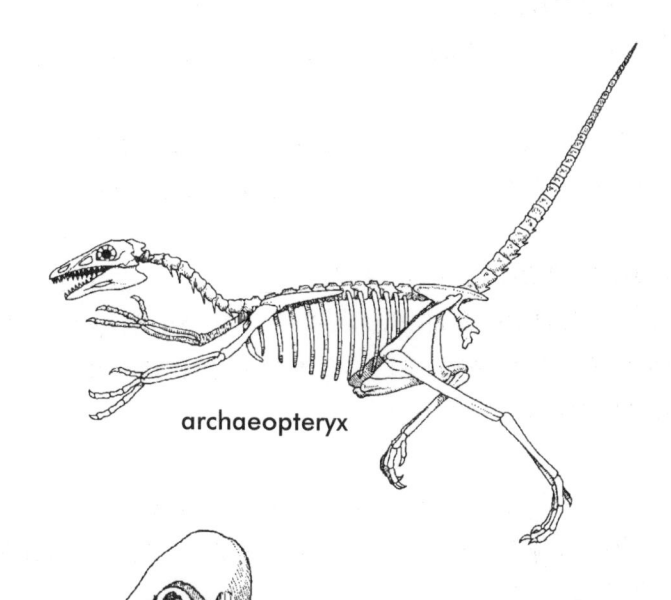

archaeopteryx

How the small dinosaurs were like birds:

1 Their legs went straight down from their hips.

2 They had 3 toes that pointed forward.
The middle toe was the longest.

crow

3 Many of their bones were like the bones of modern birds.

What do you think? Maybe you will grow up to be a paleontologist and solve this mystery.

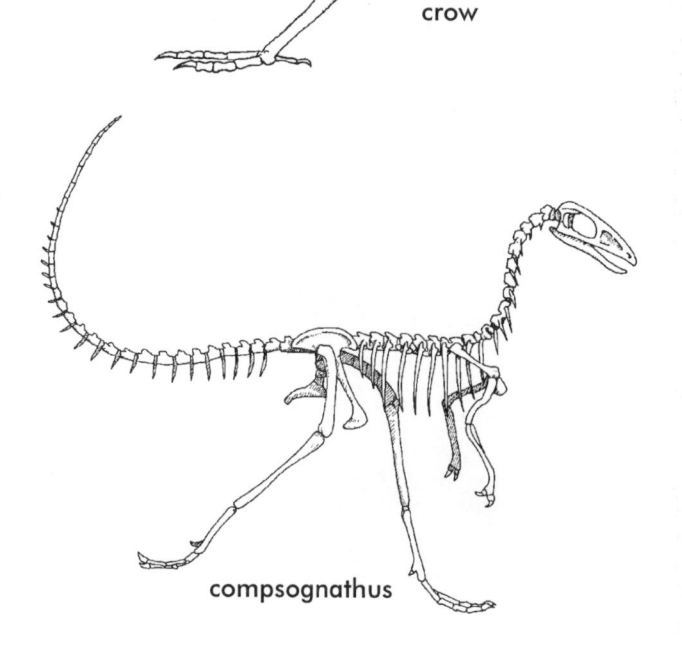

compsognathus

Note: Protoceratops was one of the dinosaurs whose eggs have been found. Have children cut out the pictures and paste them in the correct order on a separate sheet of paper to show the life cycle of the dinosaur.

| 1 | 2 A Dinosaur Is Born | 3 | 4 |

A Dinosaur Is Born

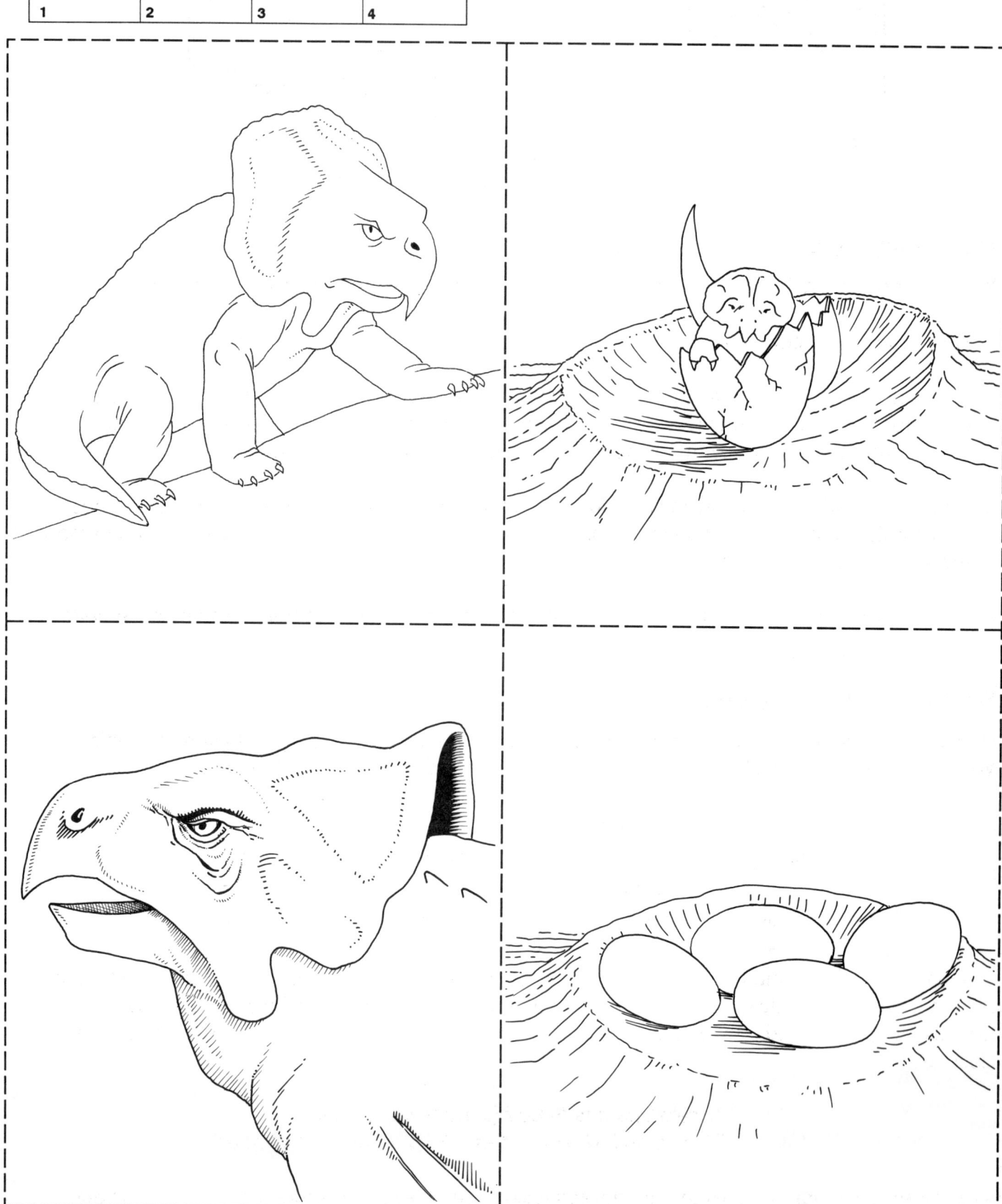

© 1996 Evan-Moor Corp.   12   Dinosaurs

Language Activities

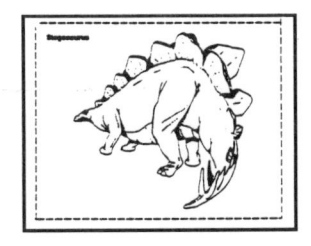

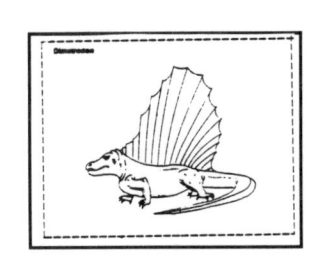

How Many Syllables Do You Hear?

You will need to teach the names of the prehistoric animals before beginning this activity.

1. Reproduce the picture cards on pages 16-19. Glue them to tag and laminate.

2. Show the cards one at a time to your students. Ask if they know its name. Pronounce each name for them if they don't know it. Once they are comfortable with the names, explain that you are going to count how many parts or syllables each word contains.

3. Begin by showing them how to listen for (or clap) the number of syllables in their own names. Begin with student names containing one syllable, two syllables, and so on, until you have tried the longest name in class.

4. Show a card, name the animal, and have students count out the number of syllables. Repeat with each card.

Sentences that Describe

Brainstorm to create a vocabulary of words children can use in describing prehistoric animals. Write these words on a chart or the chalkboard. Ask for additional words they might use.

large	strong	bumpy	sharp
gigantic	fast	smooth	long
scaly	small	quick	agile
dangerous	tall	furry	heavy

Using the cards from the previous activity, select a picture card. Have your students describe the picture. (Model the activity if this is a new experience for your students.) Do several cards for practice. Then ask students to choose one prehistoric animal and to write a sentence or two to describe it.

Triceratops has three big horns on its head.
This smooth dinosaur has a long tail and a little head.

Variation: Ask students to write a paragraph telling what they know about a specific prehistoric animal, describing what it looked liked and some of its behaviors.

© 1996 Evan-Moor Corp.   Dinosaurs EMC 253

Alike and Different

Show two picture cards. Ask your students to tell how the two prehistoric animals are alike. Begin with dinosaurs that are very similar. After some practice, increase the degree of differences.

Show two cards, and ask you students to tell how the prehistoric animals are different. Begin with very clear differences. After practice, increase the degree of similarity.

Categories

Display several picture cards. Have children group the cards according to set categories. The difficulty of the categories you select will depend on the ability of your students. You might have children group the cards in one of these ways:

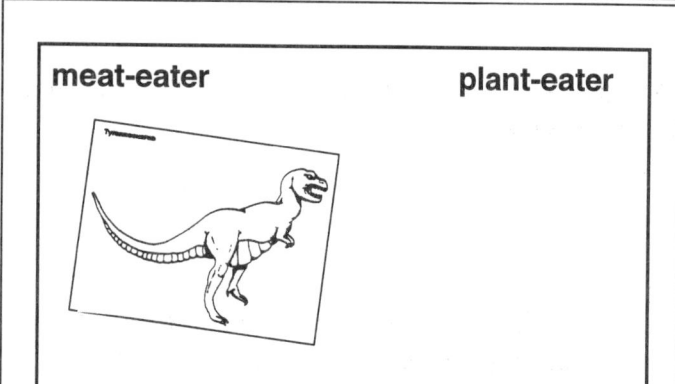

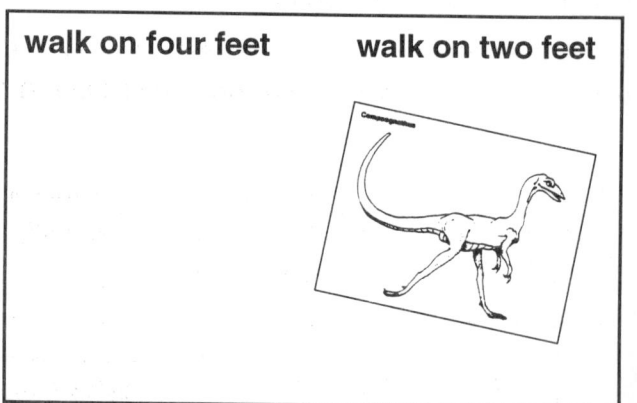

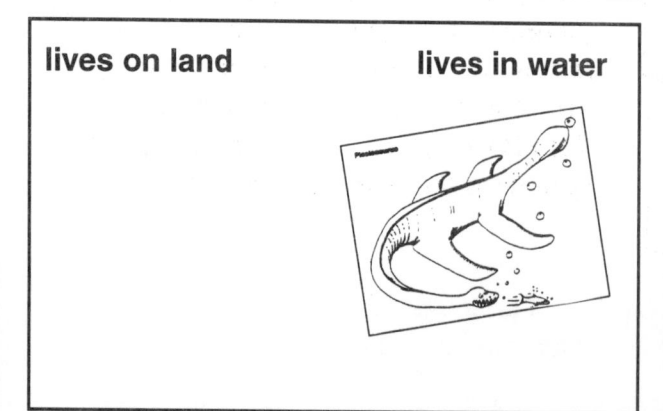

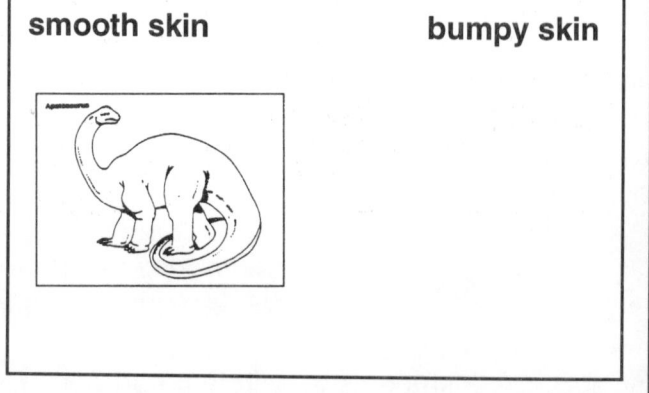

meat-eater plant-eater	walk on four feet walk on two feet
lives on land lives in water	smooth skin bumpy skin

© 1996 Evan-Moor Corp. 14 Dinosaurs EMC 253

Find the Missing Dinosaur

Use the prehistoric animal cards to practice visual memory. Display several cards. Discuss what each card shows. Have your students close their eyes as you remove one card. They open their eyes and try to decide which card has been removed.

Make the activity more difficult by changing the order of the cards instead of removing one. Display several cards. Discuss what each card shows and its order in the row. Have your students close their eyes as you rearrange the cards. Have them open their eyes and try putting the cards back into the original order.

Dinosaur Concentration

Reproduce two copies of each card you plan to include in the game. Start with a small number of pairs until your students have developed some skill at the game.

Lay the cards out upside down in rows. The first player turns over two cards. If the cards are the same, the player keeps the two cards. If the cards are different, the player turns them over and tries to remember where they are on his\her next turn. The next player then takes a turn. The game continues until all pairs have been matched.

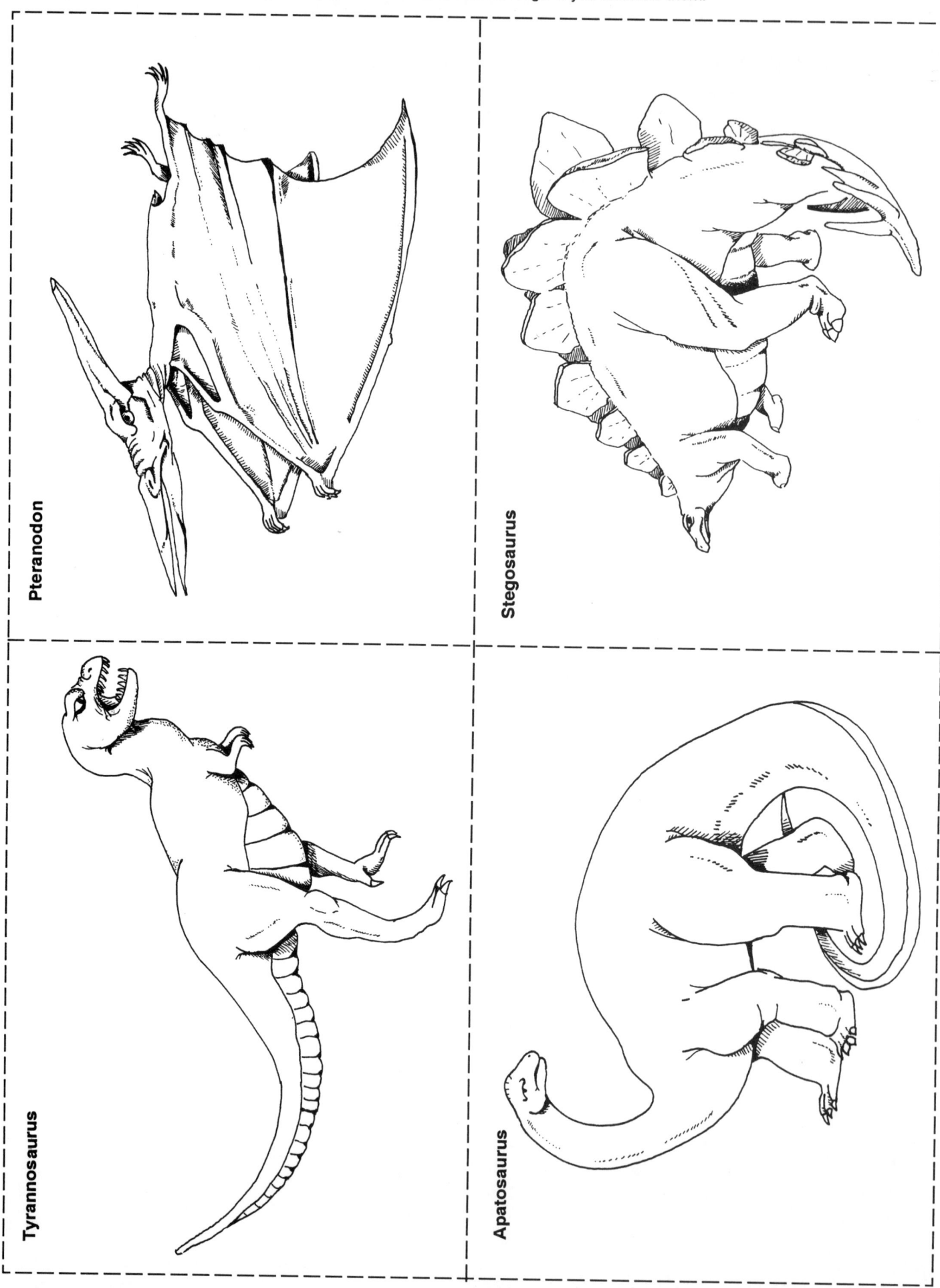

Note: Reproduce these cards on tag or card stock. The cards will last longer if you laminate them.

Pteranodon

Stegosaurus

Tyrannosaurus

Apatosaurus

© 1996 Evan-Moor Corp.

Dinosaurs

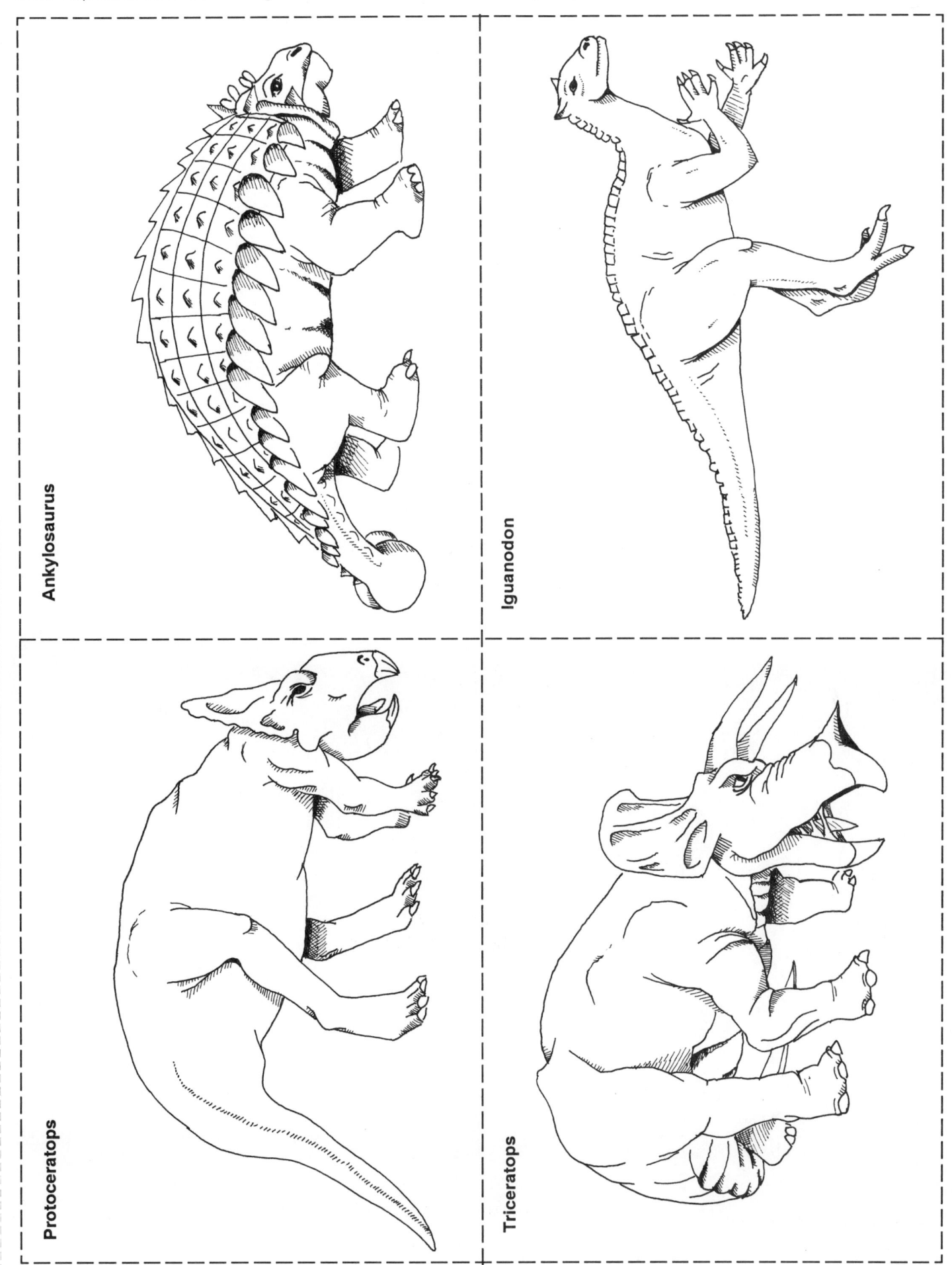

Note: Reproduce these cards on tag or card stock. The cards will last longer if you laminate them.

Ankylosaurus

Iguanodon

Protoceratops

Triceratops

© 1996 Evan-Moor Corp. 17 Dinosaurs

Note: Reproduce these cards on tag or card stock. The cards will last longer if you laminate them.

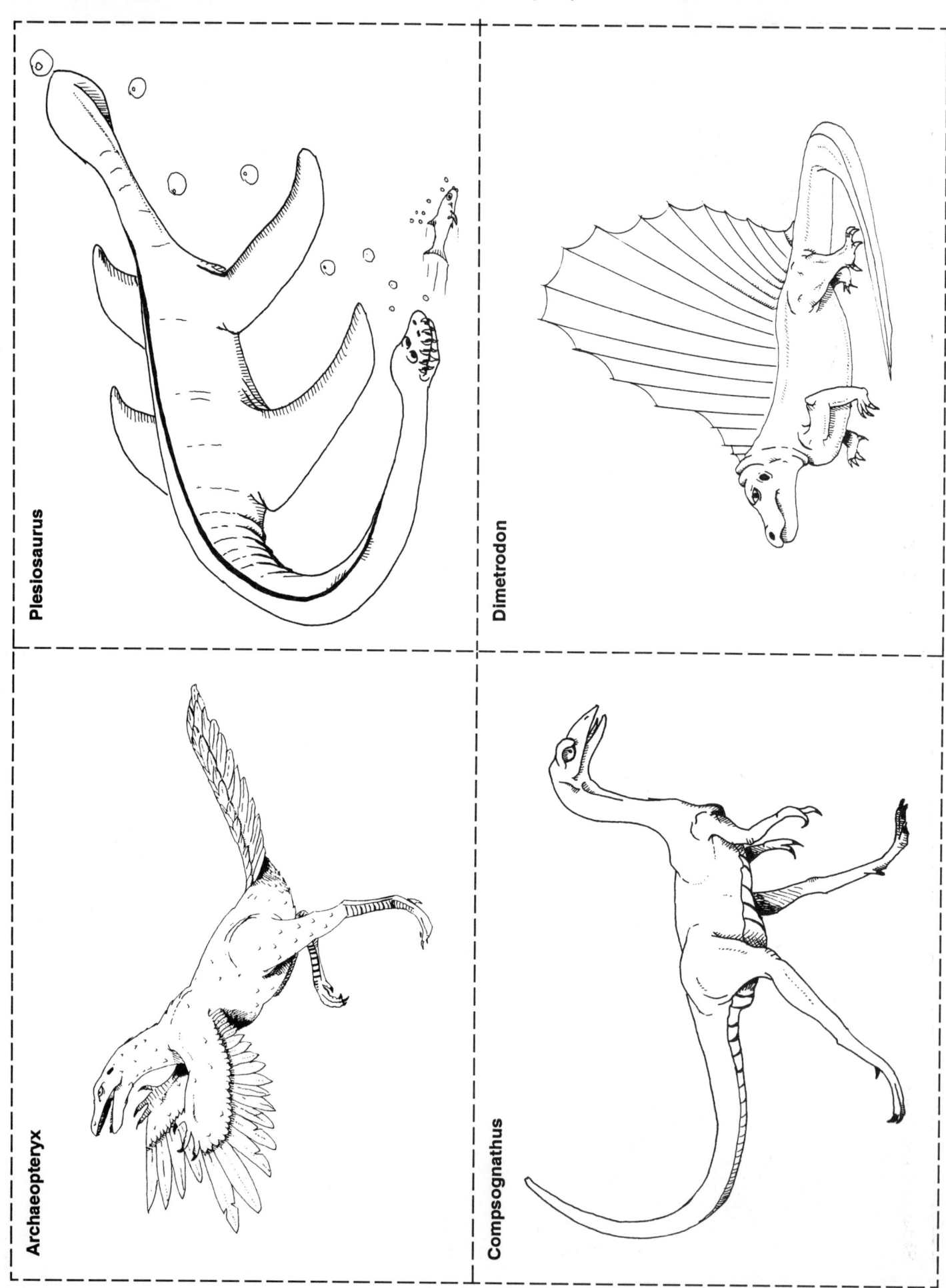

Plesiosaurus

Dimetrodon

Archaeopteryx

Compsognathus

© 1996 Evan-Moor Corp.

Dinosaurs

Note: Reproduce these cards on tag or card stock. The cards will last longer if you laminate them.

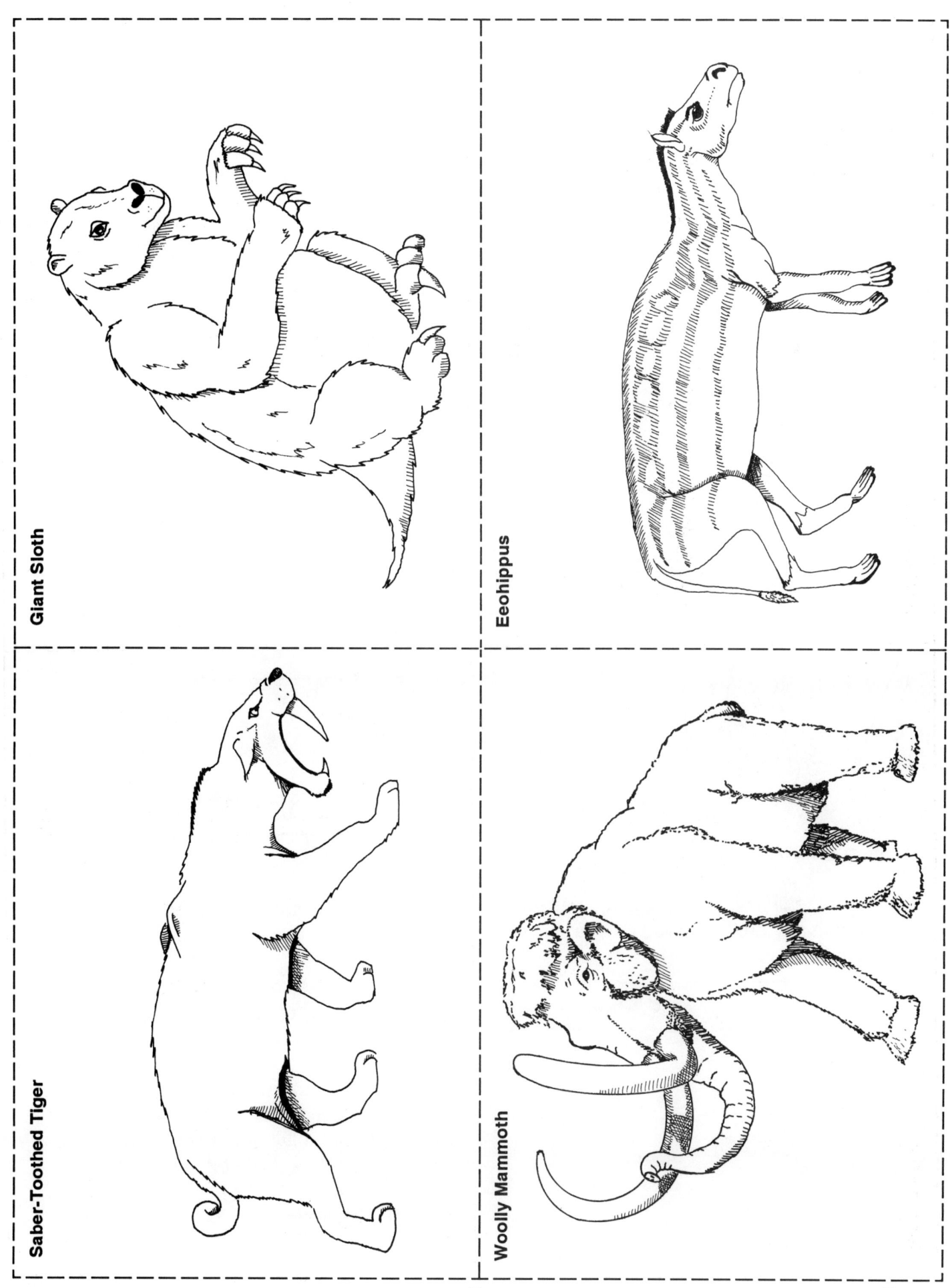

Giant Sloth

Eeohippus

Saber-Toothed Tiger

Woolly Mammoth

© 1996 Evan-Moor Corp. 19 Dinosaurs

Dinosaur Bulletin Board

Create a giant dinosaur bulletin board following the steps below. Use the dinosaur as a place to display children's work and as a background for dinosaur center activities. Place tables in front of the completed bulletin board to use for the center activities.

Steps to follow:

1. Cut out the following parts as large as you can from any bright-colored butcher paper to fill your bulletin board.

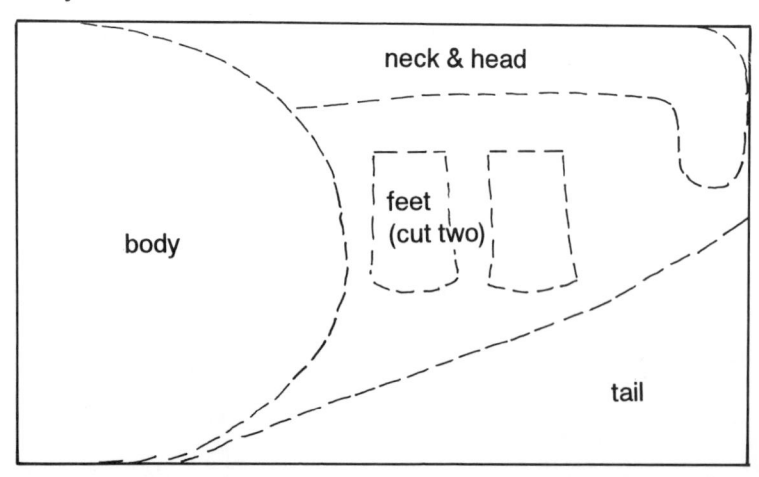

2. Add details to the head and feet with a black marking pen.

3. Pin grass cut from green construction paper along the bottom of the bulletin board.

4. Pin or staple the pieces to the bulletin board. The tail may be placed flat or may be curved around to add a three-dimensional look.

5. Cut letters from black construction paper to spell "We love dinosaurs!"

© 1996 Evan-Moor Corp.   20   Dinosaurs EMC 253

Dinosaur Centers

Dinosaur Library

Collect all the dinosaur books you can find that seem appropriate for your students. Place the books on the table in front of your dinosaur bulletin board.

Find the Bones

Fill a box with sand. Bury bones (chicken bones, pork chop bones, etc.) in the sand. One or more children are to "dig" for the bones. You can extend the activity by having cards with pictures of the animals whose bones are buried so the child can match the bone to the animal from which it came.

This can be made even more challenging for older students by burying a whole chicken carcass. (You can get heads and feet from your butcher.) They find all of the bones and try to place them together in approximately the correct position.

Fossils

Put out any actual fossils you have with a magnifying glass so children can experience them firsthand.

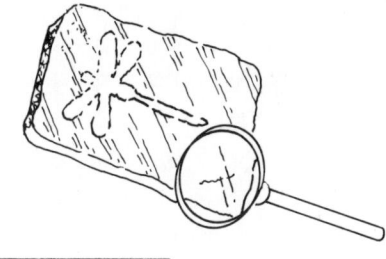

Concentration

Put out a set of the cards you made for the games on page 15 for children to use when working at the dinosaur center. Run the cards on tag and laminate them for longer use.

Categories

Put out a box of plastic objects (dinosaurs, modern animals, people, vehicles, etc.) for children to place into categories. Using construction paper or colored tag, make a set of cards containing the name of the categories and a drawing of an object that would be placed in each set. For example, if the categories were **Now** and **Long Ago** you might make cards that look like this:

Other categories you might use:
- living things - nonliving things
- animals - people - vehicles
- real - make-believe

Tell a Dinosaur Story

Put out a set of toy dinosaurs for children to manipulate as they make up a dinosaur adventure. Children may do this individually or working in pairs. Older children may want to write their adventure down on paper.

Dinosaur Puzzles and Riddles

Put out any dinosaur board games, cards, or puzzles you purchased.

Reproduce:
- the riddles on page 44
- the crossword puzzle on page 45
- the jigsaw puzzle on page 46

Put copies of each activity in your center.
Put a copy of the answers to each puzzle in an envelope pinned to the center board to make the activities self-checking.

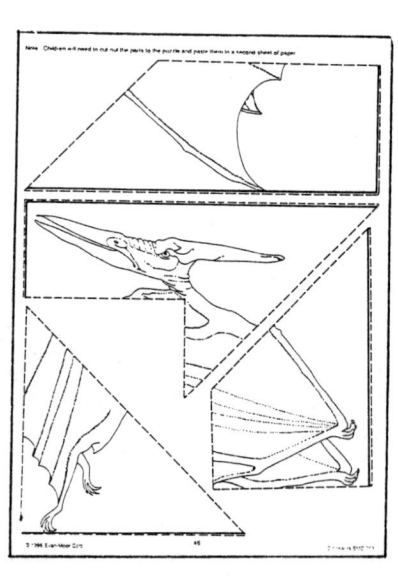

© 1996 Evan-Moor Corp.   Dinosaurs EMC 253

Dinosaur Math

One Hundred Dinosaurs

Have your students work together to draw 100 dinosaurs. (Or reproduce the dinosaurs on page 27 enough times to make one hundred.)

Use the dinosaurs in various ways.

1. Write a numeral from 1 to 100 on each dinosaur. Mix the dinosaurs up and ask students to put them in sequential order.

2. Have students count out sets of ten dinosaurs. Then have them count the sets by tens. (You can have them do the same with fives and twos.)

3. Use the numbered dinosaurs to practice finding the missing number. Display a series of dinosaurs. Ask students to determine which number/numbers are missing.

How Tall Was It?
A Measuring and Graphing Activity

Divide students into small groups. Give each group the name of a dinosaur. Their job is to find out its height and then to measure out a piece of adding machine tape the same length. They write the name of the dinosaur and its height on the strip of paper.

Pin the adding machine paper strips up on the classroom wall (you may need to go around a corner) to create a bar graph. When the graph is completed, ask questions requiring students to read the information on the graph.

Reproduce page 25. Read and discuss the page, then send it home as a homework activity.

First, Second, Third

Make a set of ten dinosaurs in different colors or patterns. Use these dinosaurs to practice ordinal positions.

Lay out the ten dinosaurs. Point to one dinosaur and ask "Which dinosaur am I touching?" Repeat with each of the dinosaurs. Then select a child to come up and touch the dinosaur you name.

Make a set of cards containing the ordinal number words. Show each card and read it with your students. Select a child to place the card with the correct dinosaur in the line. Repeat until all cards have been placed. Then mix up the cards, pass them out, and have children place them on the dinosaurs again.

Dinosaur Computation

Use the one hundred dinosaurs as manipulatives as students practice various forms of computation. Use the dinosaurs to figure out the answers to equations or word problems.

Examples:
Three protoceratops eggs hatched in the morning. Five hatched in the afternoon. How many baby hatchlings are there?

Twelve triceratops were eating. Eight stopped eating and went away. How many triceratops were still eating?

There were five groups of dinosaurs near the lake. Six dinosaurs were in each group. How many dinosaurs were near the lake?

Dinosaur Eggs

Use this activity with students who are just beginning addition and subtraction. Reproduce the mother protoceratops and her eggs on page 28.

Display the mother dinosaur. Lay out several eggs and ask questions such as the following. Manipulate the eggs to prove the answers.

"How many eggs has the mother dinosaur laid?"
"If she lays two more eggs, how many eggs will there be?"
"If three eggs hatch, how many eggs will be left in her nest?"
"I see two eggs. How many more will the dinosaur have to lay to make five?"

Continue asking questions as you add or subtract eggs. Extend the activity by writing each equation on the chalkboard as you do it.

How Tall? How Long?

Some dinosaurs were so big it is difficult to imagine how tall or how long they really were. Other dinosaurs were very small. Use string and a measuring tape to see how big or how small these dinosaurs were.

Would a triceratops fit into your living room?

1 Triceratops were about 25 feet (7.5 meters) long. Measure a piece of string that long. Stretch the string the longest way in your living room. Could a triceratops fit into the room?

2 Triceratops were nine and a half feet (3 meters) tall. Measure a piece of string that long. Ask an adult to help you see if the string reaches from the ceiling to the floor. Could a triceratops stand up in your living room?

What can you find in your house that is as tall as these dinosaurs? (Sizes can be approximate.)

1. Compsognathus
   1 foot tall (30 cm tall)

2. Velociraptor
   6 feet tall (180 cm tall)

3. Protoceratops
   2 1/2 feet tall (45 cm tall)

© 1996 Evan-Moor Corp.   Dinosaurs EMC 253

Note: Reproduce the geometric shapes on page 29 to use with this activity.

Geometric Shapes

Show each geometric shape to your students. Discuss what it is called and how many sides and corners it has.

Build one of the following dinosaurs on a bulletin board, overhead projection screen, or on a flannel board. Start with a simple dinosaur and work up to more complicated ones.

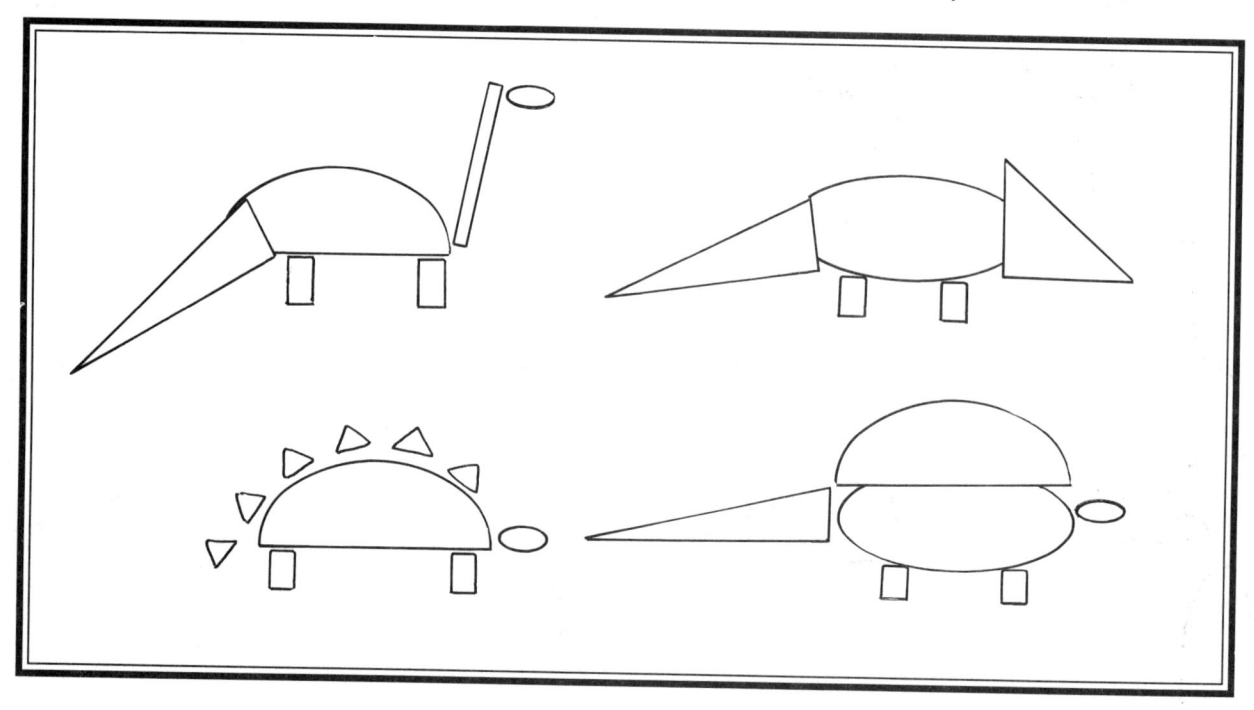

- Ask students to identify each shape they see.

- Give shapes to students and ask them to copy the dinosaur you have made.

- Give shapes to students and have them create their own dinosaurs pasting the pieces to a sheet of construction paper. Have them make a list of the kinds and number of pieces they used in their dinosaur.

   For example:
   1 big oval
   1 small oval
   2 rectangles
   1 long triangle

Extension:
Give each geometric shape a numerical value. Make a chart showing these values. Ask students to add up the total value of their dinosaur.

© 1996 Evan-Moor Corp.   Dinosaurs EMC 253

Note: Reproduce these dinosaurs to use with the activities on pages 23 and 24.

© 1996 Evan-Moor Corp. Dinosaurs EMC 253

Note: Reproduce these dinosaurs to use with the activities on pages 23 and 24.

Mother Dinosaur and Eggs

© 1996 Evan-Moor Corp. Dinosaurs EMC 253

Note: Reproduce these patterns to use with the activity on page 26.

© 1996 Evan-Moor Corp. 29 Dinosaurs EMC 253

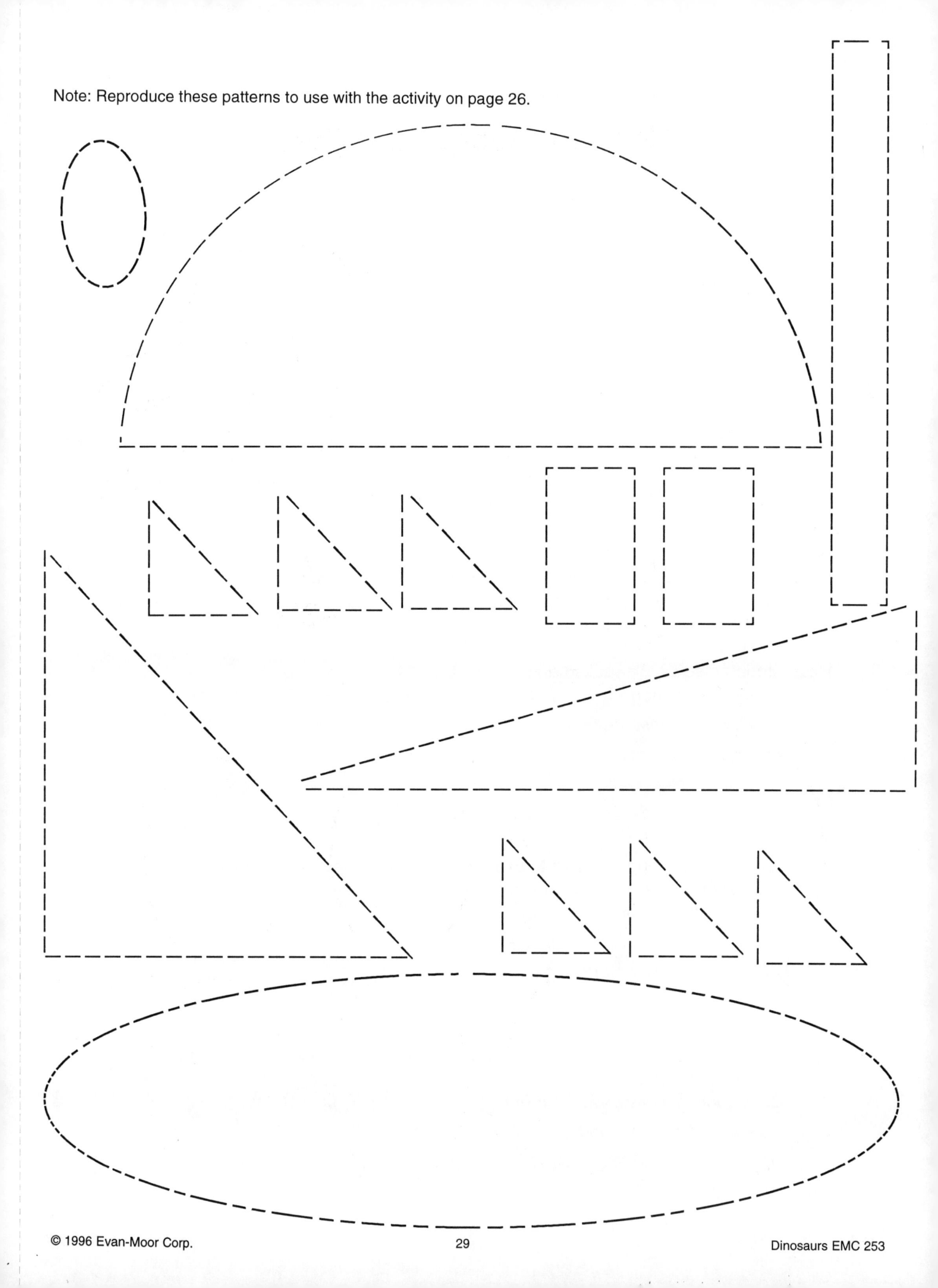

Dinosaurs at Play

Walk Like a Dinosaur

You will need a lot of moving room to do this activity. Have students scatter around the designated area at least a little more than an arm's length apart. Give a direction for a prehistoric animal movement. Students do the movement until you say "freeze." Give a new movement direction.

- Have students do simple movements.

    fly like Pteranodon

    run like Tyrannosaurus

    swim like Diplodocus

    creep like Ankylosaurus

    stretch like Apatosaurus

- Add a direction requiring students to use the information they have learned about these animals in order to do the movement.

    move like Tyrannosaurus looking for food

    move like Triceratops escaping from danger

    show Apatosaurus munching the top of a fern tree

    show Pteranodon landing

- Challenge students to come up with movements to answer these questions about imaginary situations.

    How would a legless dinosaur move?

    How would a two-legged dinosaur carry something?

    How would a four-legged dinosaur carry something?

    How would a dinosaur button its coat?

Dinosaur Tag

Set perameters for the playing area (stay on grass, only on the blacktop, etc.) and rules for tagging (a light tap, no grabbing, etc.) for this tag game.

Choose one child to be a hungry *Tyrannosaurus*. Everyone else is "food." When Tyrannosaurus catches its meal, that person becomes the new "hungry dinosaur."

Follow the Maiasaura

This is a "dinosaur" version of *Follow the Leader*.

Maiasaura means "good mother lizard." Maiasaura took care of their babies. Select someone to be the adult maiasaur. This person will be lead the "babies" around, showing them what to do. The rest of the class are the maiasaura "babies" who must do what the leader does.

Dinosaur Dash

Divide the class into teams of dinosaurs that ran around on two legs (allosaurus, tyrannosaurus, etc.). Mark two lines (distance apart will depend on the size of your students). Teams line up behind one line. At the sound of the starting whistle, the first person on each team runs to the next line and returns. When the first runner touches his/her hand, that person runs. This continues until everyone on one team has had a turn. (If you don't want to have competitive teams, have everyone pick out a dinosaur name and run all at the same time just for the exercise.)

© 1996 Evan-Moor Corp.   31   Dinosaurs EMC 253

Note: The activities with this story can be used on three separate days or can be incorporated into one longer session.

Patrick's Dinosaurs
by Carol Carrick

Day 1

Read **Patrick's Dinosaurs**.

Help your students recall what happened in the story by asking questions such as:
- Where were Patrick and Hank when they started talking about dinosaurs?
- What happened to Patrick every time his brother names a dinosaur?
- How could Diplodocus stay under water for so long?
- What happened to Patrick's dinosaurs when his brother said they lived millions of years ago?

Day 2

Read **Patrick's Dinosaurs**.

As you read each section, have your children explain what frightened Patrick about that dinosaur. Provide time for your students to discuss how they would react if they met a dinosaur on the street.

Patrick's fears were about something that didn't even exist. As soon as he knew that dinosaurs have been dead for millions of years, he was no longer frightened. See if your students can describe a time they were afraid of something that turned out not to even exist. This type of discussion may be too difficult for your younger students. If this is so, just have them discuss their fears in more general terms.

Have children draw a picture of something that used to frighten them. Then write about it, explaining how they overcame their fear.

Day 3

Read **Patrick's Dinosaurs**.

Have students look carefully at each dinosaur illustrated in the story, and then describe the size and special features of each dinosaur. Let children paint their favorite dinosaurs on large sheets of paper. When the dinosaurs are dry, cut them out and pin them to a large bulletin board.

Can you find the eight prehistoric animals hiding here? Number them.

Prehistoric Fun

© 1996 Evan-Moor Corp. 33 Dinosaurs EMC 253

Note: The activities with this story can be used on three separate days or can be incorporated into one longer session.

Fossils Tell of Long Ago
by Aliki

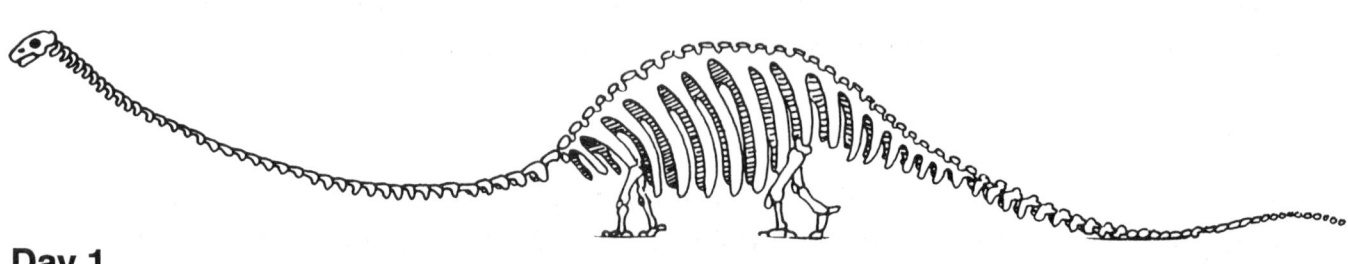

Day 1

Read Fossils Tell of Long Ago.

Help children recall information from the story by asking questions such as:

- What do scientists find that tell them about dinosaurs?
- Do scientists ever find whole animals?
- What are some of the places scientistis find fossils?
- Do scientists ever find fossils of plants that lived long ago?
- Where could you go to see fossils?

Explain what these words mean to help your children have a clearer understanding of the story.

fossil
scientist
prehistoric
extinct

Day 2

Read **Fossils Tell of Long Ago**.

Make your own "fossil" prints. In the book, it explains how students can make their own handprints in clay. You can also make prints of bones, shells, and leaves that children collect and bring to class.

Display these clay "fossil" prints on a table. Place a label by each imprint.

Day 3

Read **Fossils Tell of Long Ago**.

Spend some time studying the illustrations.
Do the fossil activity on page 38 with students.

© 1996 Evan-Moor Corp.   Dinosaurs EMC 253

Fossils

What Is a Fossil?

Fossils are the hardened remains of animals or plants that lived long, long ago. Some dinosaur fossils are prints left after the animals parts decay. There are fossils of whole skeletons and nests of dinosaur eggs. Bones, teeth, and footprints and prints of skin have all been found.

How Is a Fossil Made?

After the animal died, all of the soft parts decayed and disappeared. The hard parts like bones and teeth remained lying on the ground. Some of the bones were quickly covered with sand, mud, or water.

Over a long, long time, minerals would seep in and take the place of the bone. What was left was a rock in the same shape as the bone. This rock is what we call a fossil.

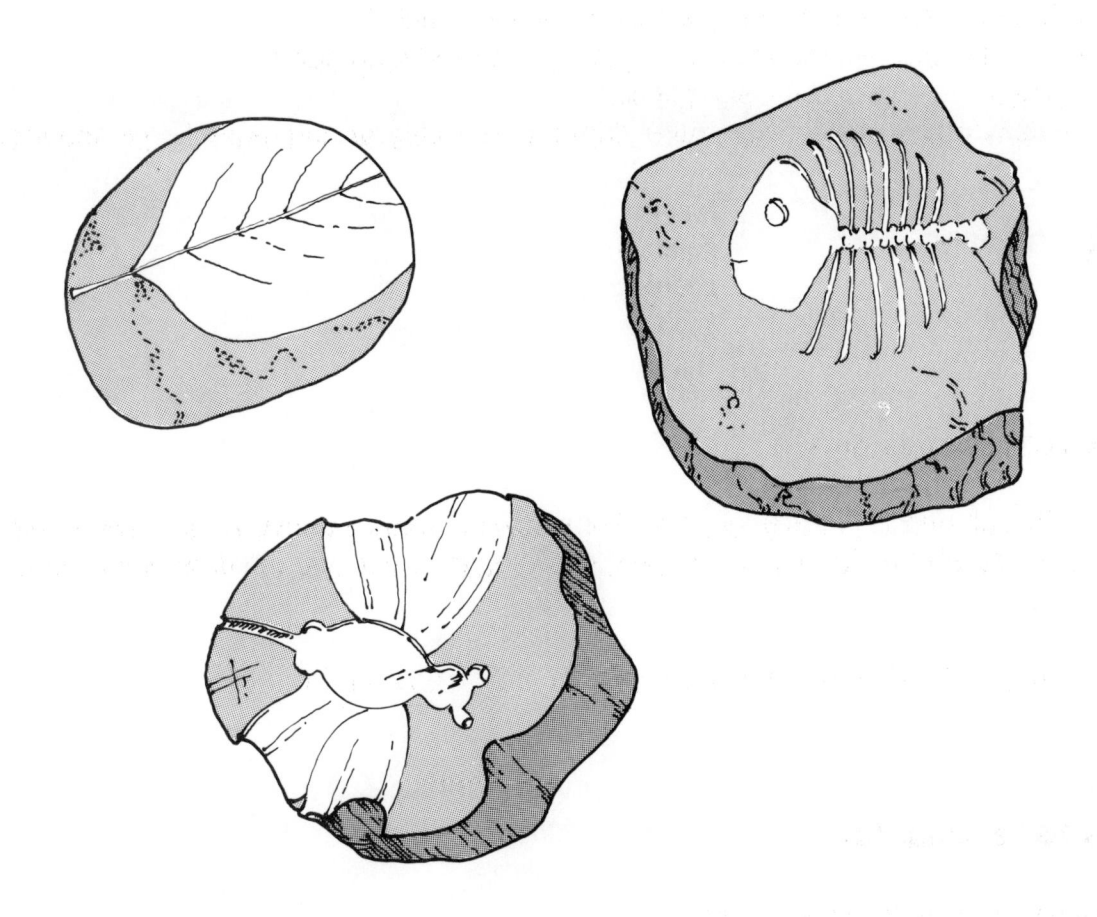

Note: You will need the clean bones of a chicken to do this exploration. You can get chicken heads and feet at your grocery meat counter. You may want to provide more than one chicken carcass so several groups can work on the skeletons.

Be a Paleontologist

Finding dinosaur bones is only the first step. The paleontologist has to study the bones. One job is to try to fit the pieces together. You can try this yourself.

First you need bones. Ask your parents to save the bones the next time you have chicken for dinner. You will need their help to clean the bones.

1 Scrape off any scraps of meat.

2 Boil the bones for an hour in soapy water.

3 Rinse the bones in clear hot water. Set them out to dry.

Now comes the interesting part. Try to lay the bones out in the correct places. Look at each bone. Ask yourself "What kind of bone is this?" "Where should it go?" Good luck! Remember, scientists don't always get it right the first time.

Big Old Bones
A Dinosaur Tale
By Carol Carrick

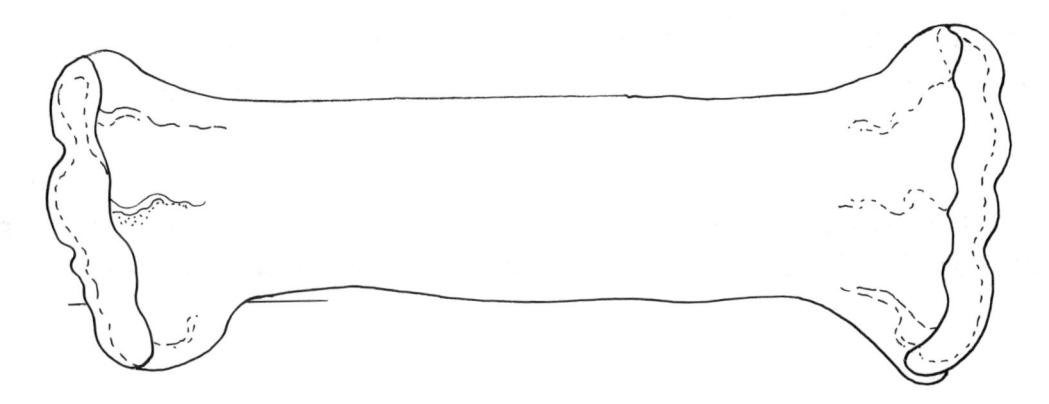

Day 1

Read **Big Old Bones.**

Help your children recall events from the story by asking questions such as:

- Where did the Professor find the big bones?
- Did he know what kind of animal the bones belonged to?
- What did he do with the bones?
- What did he ask his wife to make?
- Could a dinosaur have looked like the one in this story?

Day 2

Read **Big Old Bones**.

Help your children do some thinking about dinoaurs by asking questions such as:

- How do we know that there ever were dinosaurs?
- What would you do if you found giant-sized bones in your backyard?
- Were all dinosaurs huge? (Show Side One of the poster and look at the difference in sizes between the tiny Compagnathus and the other dinosaurs shown.)

Brainstorm to think of really big animals that are living today. Have your students decide if any of these animals are as big as the really big dinosaurs.

Day 3

Read **Big Old Bones**.

Use Side One of the poster to initiate a discussion about what scientist can tell from dinosaur fossils they find and what they cannot tell. Then go back to the final illustrations in the book to see one more time the amazing covering the Professor put on his discovery.

Make Fossil Bones

These will not really be fossils. It would take millions of years to turn your bones into fossils. This just shows you how it might happen.

Fossil Bones

You need:
- plaster of Paris
- water
- stick for stirring
- measuring cup
- large milk carton
- bones (clean chicken or beef bones)

Use these to make layers in the "rock" where you will put your fossil:
- fine sand
- coarse sand
- small gravel
- fine bark chips (or you can use just sand if that is all you have)

Steps:
1. Cut the top off of the milk carton.

2. Put a layer of each of these in the carton: fine sands, coarse sand, gravel, bark chips. After your carton is half full, put in your bones or shells. Cover them with more layers of your materials. You may make more than one layer of a material.

3. Mix the plaster of Paris. Pour it into the milk carton until all the layers are covered. (Lift the carton and tap it on the table to help the plaster fill in all the spaces.) Let it sit until the plaster is dry.

4. Tear away the milk carton. Look at the layers. Do you see any of your "fossils" sticking out?

5. Break open your "rock" and find your fossils.

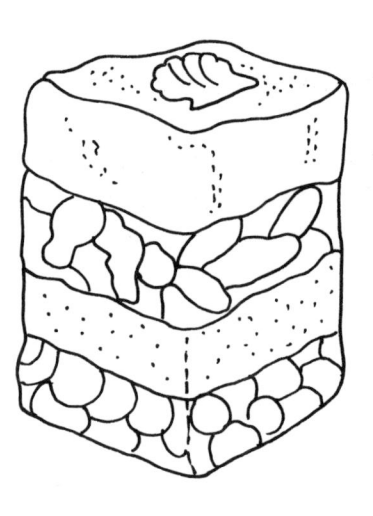

Three-Dimensional Dinosaurs

Children can make 3-D dinosaurs from many different types of materials. You need to choose the technique that is most appropriate for the developmental level of your students.

Clay Dinosaurs

Give each child a lump of clay. You may use regular clay which does not harden, self-hardening clay, or clay which can be fired if you have access to a kiln.

Encourage your students to "pinch" and "pull" the clay to create their dinosaurs. Pieces added on are apt to fall off.

Aluminum Foil Dinosaurs

Crumple sheets of aluminum foil into the shape of a dinosaur. Details can be added with permanent ink marking pens.

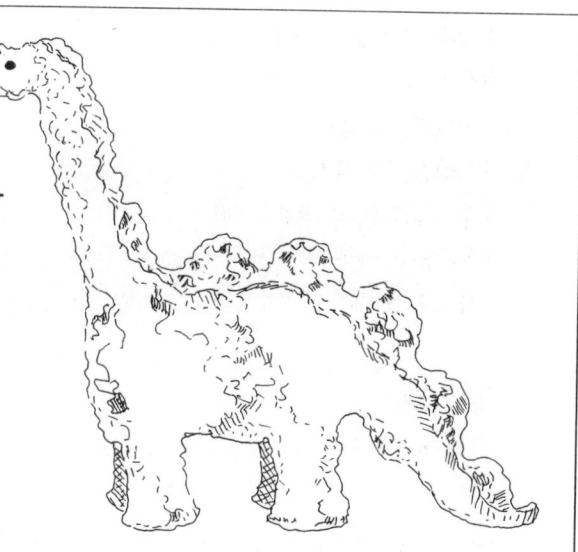

Dinosaur Skeletons

Give each child several art pipe cleaners cut into various lengths. Children twist the pipe cleaners together to create their dinosaur skeleton.

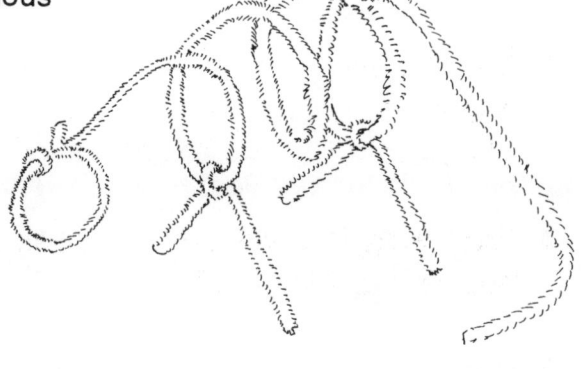

© 1996 Evan-Moor Corp.   Dinosaurs EMC 253

Note: The activities with this story can be used on three separate days or can be incorporated into one longer session.

The Magic School Bus
In the Time of the Dinosaurs
by Joanna Cole

Day 1

Read ***The Magic School Bus: In the Time of the Dinosaurs***

Discuss with students what they learned about dinosaurs from this story. Write the information on a large chart. Post it in the classroom. Add other information as you read the book again on other occasions.

Begin a class "Dinosaur Dictionary." Use the form on page 41 to create the pages. List the important words about dinosaurs from the story. Give each child (or partners) a copy of the form and one word from the list. They are to explain the word and to illustrate it, if possible. Post the completed forms on the board for everyone to read. Then put the pages together in alphabetical order in a three-hole binder. (This way you can add other pages as you continue to study dinosaurs.)

Day 2

Read ***The Magic School Bus: In the Time of the Dinosaurs***

Have students make their own dinosaur books. Each book should answer one question about dinosaurs. Brainstorm to create a list of possible topics.
dinosaurs lived in prehistoric times
some dinosaurs were small
some dinosaurs laid eggs in nests
some dinosaurs ate meat
some dinosaurs ate plants
prehistoric plants
how dinosaurs moved

Have students make a cover on construction paper. It should contain the title and their own name. The information should be written on pages of lined paper cut just a little smaller than the cover. Encourage students to include pictures as well as words. Attach the covers to the stories with yarn or staples. (If you use staples, cover them with tape to protect the readers' fingers.)

Day 3

Read ***The Magic School Bus: In the Time of the Dinosaurs***

Follow Ms. Frizzle's and her students' example. Set up "Dinosaur Land" in your own classroom. Include students stories, paintings, "fossils," etc. Invite parents to come and enjoy what you have done.

Dinosaur Dictionary

What does it mean?

word

Make a picture to show what your word means.

Real or Make-Believe

This is *(real or make-believe)* because:

_____
_____
_____
_____
_____
_____
_____
_____
_____

This is *(real or make-believe)* because:

_____
_____
_____
_____
_____
_____
_____
_____
_____

Long Ago - Today

Color the animals that lived long ago.
Put an X on the animals that live today.

Dinosaur Riddles

1. We use sharp pointed teeth to eat our food. Who are we?

2. I have three large horns on my head. Which dinosaur am I?

3. We are the clues scientists use to find out about dinosaurs. What are we?

4. I was the first flying animal with feathers. Who am I?

5. I am the scientist who studies fossils. Who am I?

6. I am a prehistoric flying reptile. Who am I?

Word Box

| archaeopteryx | paleontologist | meat-eaters |
| fossils | pteranodon | triceratops |

Note: Reproduce these cards and the game board on page 48 on tagboard and laminate them. Provide small plastic dinosaurs or buttons to use as playing pieces. Children pick a card and move the number of spaces shown. (These cards contain simple addition and subtraction problems. You can make up cards for containing multiplication and divisions problems when your students are ready.

"Help Me Get to My Cave!"

1 + 0 =	1 - 0 =	1 + 1 =
2 + 0 =	2 - 0 =	2 - 1 =
2 + 1 =	1 + 2 =	3 - 1 =
3 - 2 =	one + one =	one + two =
two + one =	one + zero =	two + zero =
two - one =	three - one =	three - two =

Note: Follow the directions on page 47 to play this game.

Help me get to my cave!

start

finish

© 1996 Evan-Moor Corp.

Dinosaurs